D0118874

# Nelson Mandela

## *Leader Against Apartheid*

### Benjamin Pogrund

**BLACKBIRCH™**
**PRESS**

**THOMSON**

**GALE**

San Diego • Detroit • New York • San Francisco • Cleveland
New Haven, Conn. • Waterville, Maine • London • Munich

Photo Credits: Associated Press: 27, 51 (below), 58, 59; Mary Evans Picture Library: 9; Gamma Liaison: 12; International Defence and Aid Fund for Southern Africa: 4 (top and below), 7, 10 (Ben Maclennan), 11, 15, 18, 20 (top and below), 21 (Eli Weinberg), 24 (left and right), 25, 28 (Jurgen Schadelberg), 31, 33, 36, 38 (Eli Weinberg), 39, 40 (top), 45, 46 (below), 52 (Dave Hartman), 53, 57 (top and below); Alf Kumalo: 48, 49; Magnum: 16 (Eve Arnold), 19 (top and below Ian Berry), 34 and 35 (Abbas), 54-5 (G. Mendel); Peter Magubane: 23, 40 (below) 50-1, 51; Pictures by Tony Nutley from the TVS film Mandela: 43 (top and below); Spectrum Colour Library: 46 (top); Cover: CORBIS.

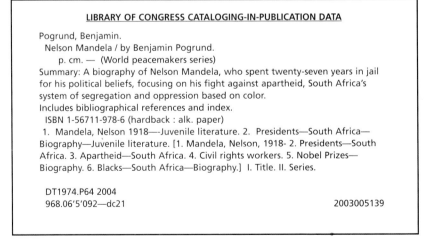

### LIBRARY OF CONGRESS CATALOGING-IN-PUBLICATION DATA

Pogrund, Benjamin.
  Nelson Mandela / by Benjamin Pogrund.
    p. cm. — (World peacemakers series)
Summary: A biography of Nelson Mandela, who spent twenty-seven years in jail for his political beliefs, focusing on his fight against apartheid, South Africa's system of segregation and oppression based on color.
Includes bibliographical references and index.
  ISBN 1-56711-978-6 (hardback : alk. paper)
  1. Mandela, Nelson 1918—Juvenile literature. 2. Presidents—South Africa—Biography—Juvenile literature. [1. Mandela, Nelson, 1918- 2. Presidents—South Africa. 3. Apartheid—South Africa. 4. Civil rights workers. 5. Nobel Prizes—Biography. 6. Blacks—South Africa—Biography.] I. Title. II. Series.

  DT1974.P64 2004
  968.06'5'092—dc21                                                      2003005139

**Printed in China**
10 9 8 7 6 5 4 3 2 1

# Contents

*Above: On February 11, 1990, after 27 years in prison, South African leader Nelson Mandela was freed. He and his wife, Winnie greeted a cheering crowd that day.*

*Right: Two months after his release from prison, Mandela gave a televised speech at one of the many events celebrating his freedom.*

# Freedom

At 4:17 P.M., Nelson Mandela walked through the gates of the prison. He raised his right hand in a clenched-fist salute. He was free.

A tense world had been waiting for Nelson Mandela. The moment of his release on Sunday, February 11, 1990, was recorded by hundreds of journalists outside South Africa's Victor Verster prison. Television cameras instantly carried the scene to an estimated 1 billion viewers around the world; broadcasters gave excited descriptions to millions of radio listeners. Reporters scribbled notes and cameras whirred for the next day's newspapers.

Never before had any released prisoner received such massive attention. Never before had so many people around the world had never waited for their first sight of a person whose name was a household word, but whose face and voice were unknown. Only that morning had the first photograph of Mandela in more than a quarter of a century appeared. Now the world wanted to see him.

The cameras showed a tall man with his hair white and face lined, but his body taut and upright. He walked smoothly and deliberately, despite his 71 years. Dressed in a smart, well-cut suit, he hardly looked like a man who had been in jail for 27 years.

This first impression of strength was confirmed two hours later when Mandela spoke to the world from city hall in Cape Town, the city near the southern tip of the African continent. His voice was firm as he began, "I greet you all in the name of peace, democracy and freedom for all."

The fact that Nelson Mandela had spent 27 years in prison for his political beliefs was reason in itself for the intense interest in him. Even more, he had repeatedly been offered release, but had steadfastly rejected it because of his commitment to his cause— the struggle for freedom for the black people of South Africa, and the destruction of apartheid.

"During my lifetime I have dedicated my life to this struggle of the African people. I have fought against white domination, and I have fought against black domination. I have cherished the ideal of a democratic and free society in which all persons live together in harmony with equal opportunities. It is an ideal which I hope to live for, and to see realized. But my lord, if needs be, it is an ideal for which I am prepared to die."

—Nelson Mandela, from his statement at the Rivonia Trial, October 1963

5

## Apartheid

Apartheid—discrimination by whites against people because of the color of their skin—has ranked as one of the great crimes of the twentieth century. The fact that the Republic of South Africa applied it on a scale unknown anywhere else—and even invented the word, apartheid brought the country into the international spotlight.

The word *apartheid*—Afrikaans for "separateness" and pronounced "apart-hite"—was first introduced to the world in 1948. The National Party, which represented Afrikaners (South Africans of European ancestry), was elected to govern South Africa and began to implement racial segregation. All whites could vote, but people with darker skin were not usually allowed to vote, even though they made up the majority of the population.

Apartheid actually began in South Africa long before 1948. It dates back to the seventeenth century, when the Netherlands was a powerful trading nation. Its Dutch East Indies Company controlled a vast commercial empire around the Indian Ocean. Voyages by sailing ships were long, arduous and dangerous, and the Dutch decided to establish a halfway refreshment station at the Cape of Good Hope, where Cape Town now stands.

On April 6, 1652, Jan van Riebeeck and 90 men landed there after a voyage from the Netherlands. Their orders were to make it possible for the company's ships "to refresh themselves with vegetables, meat, water and other necessities by which means the sick on board may be restored to health."

## Permanent settlement

The refreshment station rapidly drew more settlers from the Netherlands, as well as a group of Huguenots, Protestants who were fleeing from religious persecution in France.

As more settlers began to farm, conflict developed with the Khoikhoi, native people who moved around the countryside with their cattle

6

*The National Party took power after winning a whites-only election in 1948. These men were in the first cabinet and officially enforced the policy of apartheid—racial separateness—in South Africa.*

and sheep. The usually friendly trading between settlers and Khoikhoi degenerated as the local people fought back against the loss of their grazing lands.

It was an unequal struggle because the settlers had guns and the Khoikhoi had only bows and arrows. The Dutch began to hunt down the Khoikhoi, and often killed hundreds at a time. The same fate awaited another native people, the San or Bushmen.

Within only a few years of the start of European settlement, the future of South Africa was already decided, with white people as the overlords and people with darker skins as their servants. Intermarriage between the groups created another large group of mixed-race people.

In 1795, Great Britain occupied the Cape and brought in its own settlers. An English-speaking group of Europeans lived alongside the Dutch.

## Dislike of authority

The Dutch settlers had already developed a tradition of fighting against authority. They wanted to be left alone to do as they pleased. They resented the British presence at the Cape because their rulers were now foreigners. They became even more upset when, in 1834, Great Britain abolished slavery. Many Dutch settlers decided to leave on a Great Trek. They slowly drove their ox wagons over the mountains and across the dry veld.

They continued to farm and became known as Boers. In their desire to get away from authority, they led lonely, hard lives. They began to mistrust the outside world. Children were taught to read the Bible, but that was all they read. Their religion was the stern Calvinism developed in Europe 100 years before. They did not have slaves; but their black servants were kept in a lowly, debased state and were at the mercy of their employers. A new cheap workforce was also available to the Boers—the Bantu, whom the Boers encountered as they moved inland.

Through the first half of the nineteenth century, southern Africa was in turmoil as black tribes fought each other for land and supremacy. The first black people the settlers met—as early as 1702—were the Xhosa in the eastern part of the country. In the interior were other black peoples, including the Sotho, Pedi, and Swazi.

## Inter-Tribal Warfare

The greatest warriors were among the Zulus, however, in what is now Natal on the east coast. Shaka, an early nineteenth-century king, trained his soldiers to go barefoot by making them run over fields of thorns. He was a cruel leader who mercilessly killed those who opposed him.

The settlers and the British became part of the battles. They fought tribes themselves and set tribes against one another. Gradually, the superior firepower of the white fighters put them on top.

*Zulu warriors' fighting style could not stand up to the guns of the British army. British soldiers, such as the ones pictured, destroyed villages by setting fire to the roofs of thatched huts.*

By the time of the last great battle in 1879, when British troops broke the might of the Zulu army, many tribal people had been driven into ever-smaller areas of land, most of their cattle dead or seized. To survive, they had to take jobs on the farms of the white settlers or seek help from missionaries.

Up to this point, South Africa had consisted of a series of agricultural communities. This was changed by two discoveries that pushed the region into the industrial era.

First, in 1866, a farmer saw children playing with a stone—which proved to be a giant diamond. Word quickly spread and prospectors rushed in from all over the world. The diamonds had to be dug out of the ground, and the pattern already established on white-owned farms was carried over: Black people worked for white bosses and did the heavy manual work for little pay. To keep it that way, white miners arranged it so that only white people could get licenses to dig for and to deal in diamonds.

## City of Gold

Then, 20 years later, in 1886, even more brilliant riches were unearthed: Gold was found on a scale never known before or since. The city that grew up as fortune hunters poured in was called Johannesburg. To Zulus, it became eGoli—"City of Gold."

Many workers were needed to dig the shafts and tunnels that went deeper and deeper into the ground to reach the gold. White miners, many of whom came from Europe, made sure that they kept the skilled work and higher pay for themselves. Even though blacks earned little, poverty in the rural areas was so bad that the mines drew them like a magnet.

Even so, the mines needed still more workers and further pressures were introduced to force black men to leave their homes in the remote countryside to work in the mines. A basic method used was a "poll tax," which every black man had to pay each year or go to prison. For many, the only way to raise the money was to work outside the black tribal areas. Apartheid laws did not allow these migrant workers to bring wives and children to the city. Millions of black families were separated in this way. Men were allowed to go and work for only as long as they were needed, after which they had to return home.

## Systems of control

A bureaucracy of officials, police, prosecutors, magistrates and prison wardens gradually came into existence to direct the lives of black people. Residential segregation was already the rule: White families lived in their own suburbs in the new towns. A distance away were separate areas for black people. These places were overcrowded, poverty-stricken, and disease-ridden, without proper water or sewage facilities.

The diamond fields were under Great Britain's colonial wing. The gold bonanza, however, was in the heart of the South African Republic, one of several republics founded by the Boers after they conquered the native black people. The Boers were horrified by the influx of the white immigrants who came to seek their fortunes.

*Above: The discovery of diamonds brought the promise of riches. As thousands flocked to the new mines, a pattern of work was put firmly in place: white workers did the skilled jobs and black workers did the pick and shovel work for much less money.*

*Opposite: Sitting around a small stove to keep warm, black workers slept on concrete bunks.*

11

Not only were they foreigners, but they demanded a say in government in return for paying taxes.

## The Boer War

Tensions mounted and Great Britain intervened. In 1899, the Boer War broke out. Within a few months, the cities of Johannesburg and Pretoria had fallen to British troops. It seemed that the war was over. Still, many Boers refused to give in. They turned to commando tactics, fighting on horseback behind British lines.

Great Britain drafted 250,000 soldiers and resorted to scorched-earth tactics. They burned down Boer farmsteads and put women, children, and elderly men into concentration camps. A peace agreement was signed in 1902.

The war shaped the future. The Boers were embittered by their defeat and their suffering. They hated

*Muhandas Gandhi's tactics of nonviolent resistance to unjust laws were developed and used by the ANC when it was formed in 1912. Here, blacks lie down in the path of British Soldiers.*

Great Britain and foreign influences even more than before. Their feelings intensified as British officials tried to suppress the Boers and struck at Afrikaans, the local language that had evolved from Dutch. Children who spoke Dutch in school were forced to wear a dunce cap and stand in the corner. Despite this treatment, Boer-Afrikaners were determined to survive as a people.

Great Britain soon tried to reconcile the two main white groups—the Boers and the English-speakers, and on May 31, 1910, the Union of South Africa came into being.

Black people were by far the majority inside the Union, but Great Britain agreed with the white leaders that blacks should have only second-class status. Denied the right to vote, black people were made aliens in their own country. Mixed-race people—called "coloreds"—were shunted to the side.

Another group was also part of the population: Late in the nineteenth century, Asians had been brought from India to work in sugarcane fields in Natal, a small South African province. They and other immigrants from India became victims of racial discrimination. They were not allowed to vote and they needed permission to travel between different parts of the country.

## Birth of the ANC—1912

Resentment about their inferior status led blacks to form the South African Native National Congress, later renamed the African National Congress (ANC), two years after the Union was formed. The ANC pleaded with the government to give the black people fair treatment, but it was ignored. It sent representatives to Great Britain to beg for protection against the white government, but was spurned. The South African parliament continued to enact laws that reduced the rights of the black majority.

One of the first, and most devastating, measures the parliament took was the introduction of "job reservation," which strengthened segregation in mining. The law specified that black miners could not do skilled work nor set off explosives, a vital task. These jobs were reserved entirely for white miners.

An even more basic law, the Native Land Act of 1913, allocated more than 90 percent of the total land to the white population of 1.5 million, while less than 10 percent of the land was set aside for the 5.5 million blacks. Blacks were deprived of their land and forced to drift in misery and hopelessness. The South African black people found themselves dispossessed in the land of their birth. Later, the law was extended so that blacks could no longer buy land in the towns.

## More segregation laws

Additional laws ordered cities and towns to provide segregated residential areas for blacks. These were called "locations." Methods were refined to control black families that came to the towns. Town councils, all of which were run by whites, expelled "surplus" blacks—that is, black people whose work was not needed by whites.

At the heart of the controls was the "pass." All black men had to carry a document that noted whether they had permission to be in a certain town. Men also had to carry receipts to show that their tax payments were up to date.

Any policeman could stop a black man anywhere and demand to see his pass. If he did not have one, or if it did not have the correct official information on it, he was arrested, prosecuted, and imprisoned. More than 10 million people were prosecuted under the pass laws during the next few decades.

Laws gave the government the power to do almost anything it liked in black areas. The government could order any black person—or even an entire nation—to leave home and go somewhere else. It could order a person or group not to leave a specified place. Thus, building on the pattern of white-black relations established over the previous 250 years, the rule over black people grew tighter and more restrictive.

## Nelson Mandela is born

It was into this situation that Nelson Rolihlahla Mandela was born on July 18, 1918. In accordance with custom, he was given a European name as well as his Xhosa name, Rolihlahla, which means "one who brings trouble on himself."

His father, Henry Mphakanyiswa Gadla, was a chief—wealthy enough to own a horse and enough cattle to support four wives. He had 12 children. Nelson was the son of his third wife, Nosekeni Fanny. Nelson also had three sisters.

Mandela was born in the Transkei region of South Africa, in the small village of Qunu—a collection of beehive-shaped huts with thatch roofs known as rondavels. His mother had three huts and Mandela lived with her and his sisters. One hut was used to sleep in, another to cook in, and the third to store grain and

*The ANC was formed in 1912 to seek rights for black people in South Africa. Though they sent representatives to Britain to seek protection from the white government, they did not find any help there.*

other food. Everyone slept on mats on the ground, without pillows. His mother, as a married woman, had her own field to tend and her own cattle kraal—an enclosure for cattle made from thorn bushes.

It was a quiet, tranquil life. Qunu was a long way from any city, especially in days when local roads, if they existed at all, were unsurfaced.

Almost as soon as Nelson was old enough to walk, he was expected to help look after the family's cattle and goats. Relatives remember that he loved animals, and while herding, he would speak to each cow by name, as if it were a friend.

His mother could not read or write, but Nelson had to be educated, and he started as a pupil at the local school. He was said to be a quiet, industrious boy who did not live up to his Xhosa name. The school had classes only for younger students, and when Nelson was ten,

*Nelson Mandela was born in the Transkei region of South Africa (pictured) on July 18, 1918.*

his father died, so there was no money for further education. His father's nephew, Chief Jongintaba, took over.

In Xhosa society that was the natural thing to do. Jongintaba was the head of the Madiba clan. In terms of custom, all members of the clan were treated as part of the same family because they were all descended from the same ancestor. Mandela, or anyone else, could go to the home of any fellow Madiba, whether in the same village or in a village miles away, and know that he would be given food and shelter. In the same way, Jongintaba accepted responsibility for his clansman's education, exactly as he would have done if Nelson were his own child.

## The Great Place

In 1928, Nelson moved to the Great Place, which was the royal kraal at Mqekezweni. There, he shared a rondavel with his cousin Justice. The school was a small, rough building, and two classes were held in one room at the same time. Nelson learned English, Xhosa, geography, and history. He wrote out his lessons on slates.

Each day after school, he and Justice went to the fields to look after the cattle and to drive them back to the kraal in the evening for milking. At night, he sat around the fire as he had done at Qunu and listened to the elders of the community speak about "the good old days, before the coming of the white man." They spoke of a time when their people could move freely up and down the country, when they had their own king and government. They told tales of the wars fought by their ancestors in defense of their territory and of their acts of courage.

These were the years that formed Nelson Mandela's character and shaped his attitudes. Learning about the history of his people helped him develop a commitment to helping them.

## A celebratory feast

When Nelson graduated from primary school, the clan celebrated in the traditional manner: A sheep was slaughtered for a feast.

"Almost every African household in South Africa knows about the massacre of our people at Bulhoek [1921] in the Queenstown district when detachments of the army and police, armed with artillery machine-guns and rifles, opened fire on unarmed Africans, killing 163 persons, wounding 129, during which 95 people were arrested simply because they refused to move from a piece of land on which they lived."

—Nelson Mandela, at a conference in Ethiopia, February 1962

"We listened to Tatu Joyi and it made us angry that the British had done these things to us and ashamed that our ancestors had allowed these things to happen to them. Even then I saw that Nelson's anger was the greatest of all.

That is why he has spent his life in prison. He told the court of these things when they sentenced him. I could not be there, but I read every word he said and it was true and I heard Tatu Joyi in those words."

—Ntombizodwa, recalling Mandela's time at Mqekezweni

*Below: At age 19, Mandela was tall, good looking, and popular with women.*

Jongintaba still wanted to sponsor Nelson's education, so he sent Nelson first to Clarkebury and then to Healdtown, one of the top schools for black pupils. The white authorities made sure that there were separate schools for whites and blacks, and also separate ones for "coloreds" and Asians. The government spent at least ten times more money on white children than on blacks, and the results were obvious in the schools. Education for whites was compulsory. That was not the case for blacks, and large numbers of children never went to school at all or dropped out at an early age. Those children, like Nelson Mandela, who actually got as far as high school, belonged to a small elite.

At Healdtown, Nelson was a boarder in a dormitory that had only beds and small lockers for each boy. He was given a mattress cover that he filled with straw to make his bed.

At 6:00 A.M. each day, a wake-up bell rang. After a quick wash in cold water, Nelson had breakfast—a mug of hot water with sugar and a piece of bread. Lunch was the big meal, and he ate lots of beans with maize porridge, sometimes with a small piece of meat. Dinner was the same as breakfast. On Saturdays, Nelson could walk seven miles to the nearest village to buy fish and chips, if he could afford it.

Religion was a big part of Mandela's life at Healdtown. He had always gone to church regularly, and, at Healdtown, he took part in the prayers recited every evening. On Sundays, he went to church and to scripture lessons.

In 1938, Nelson Mandela finished his schooling. He had done so well that Jongintaba decided he should go on to college, to the South African Native College at Fort Hare, not far from Healdtown. The college was racially segregated. Most of its 300 students were blacks, but there were also "coloreds" and Asians.

Like any student, Mandela soon discovered that there was much more to college than study alone. He was tall and good-looking, especially in the three-piece suit tailored for him, and was popular with women. He took up ballroom dancing and spent a lot of time learning to waltz and foxtrot.

## Suspended from college

Living conditions at Fort Hare were more comfortable than they had been at Healdtown. Still, students complained about the poor quality of the food, and when nothing was done about it, Mandela took his first protest action: He became involved in a strike. In response, the college authorities suspended him.

Jongintaba told Mandela to apologize to the authorities so that he could return to his studies. He refused to do so.

Along with his cousin Justice, Mandela decided to run away to Johannesburg. It was hundreds of miles to the north, and to raise money to get there the two young men sold two of Jongintaba's oxen to a local trader. Jongintaba was extremely angry. He tracked the boys down and found them at the gold mine in Johannesburg where Mandela had obtained a job as a mine policeman. Jongintaba told them to return home. The two young men were evicted from the mine. Justice had to go back, but Mandela persuaded Jongintaba to let him remain in Johannesburg so that he could study law.

## Johannesburg

Johannesburg was an exciting, bewildering city to the young man, who was accustomed only to rural life and the small town of Fort Hare. He was in South Africa's premier city, which bustled with vitality.

In the northern section of the city, there were the large houses of wealthy white families, with pleasant gardens filled with trees and flowers. Not all whites lived so grandly. Even the modest houses, however, were far better than the houses of black families. For black people, life was best in townships such as Sophiatown and Alexandra, where blacks could still own land, even though these townships were crowded, squalid, and rife with crimes.

*Above, right: When
Mandela arrived in
Johannesburg, he lived in
a township where black
people were surrounded
by poverty.*

It was 1941 when 23-year-old Nelson Mandela arrived in Johannesburg. World War II had started two years earlier, and South Africa had joined with Great Britain against Nazi Germany.

The war stimulated industry. There was suddenly a need for factories to produce everything from armored cars to boots and cigarettes for soldiers. Workers were wanted and blacks streamed in from the reserves. The influx of people swelled the already crowded cities.

Now, however, black people could dream about the future. It was a time of hope. With war under way against the Nazis, talk of democracy was in the air. The government wanted to get black men to join the army—although they would not be allowed to carry weapons—and held out the possibility of a new deal for blacks in the postwar era.

Meanwhile, the ANC had had an erratic existence during the preceding 30 years, swinging between popularity and decline. It had been in a low state when, in 1940, a new ANC president was elected. He was Dr. A.B. Xuma, a doctor who had studied in Great Britain, the United States, and Hungary. He changed the ANC into a modern, political movement.

*Mandela wore national dress on one of the occasions he was on trial.*

## Marriage

Mandela enjoyed the headiness and energy of Johannesburg. He lived in Alexandra and struggled to survive on the little money he had. Resuming his studies, he graduated with a bachelor of arts degree by correspondence and trained with a white lawyer, Lazer Sidelsky. The lawyer took a keen interest in the progress of the young Mandela, and became like an older brother to him.

It was in Johannesburg that Nelson Mandela met Walter Sisulu, a man who, with Mandela, would go on to become one of South Africa's leaders. Sisulu and Mandela got along well; it was the start of a life-long friendship.

Sisulu had an enormous influence on Mandela's life, and it began on a personal level. Mandela went

•••••••••••••••••••••••••

"Groomed from child-hood for respectability, status and sheltered living, he was now thrown into the melting-pot of urban survival."

—Mary Benson, South African author, on Mandela's arrival in Johannesburg

•••••••••••••••••••••••••

to stay with the Sisulu family in nearby Orlando. There, Sisulu introduced him to a cousin, Evelyn Mase, a nurse from the Transkei.

Romance blossomed between Evelyn and Mandela, and they married in 1944. There was no money for a traditional wedding feast, nor could they find anywhere to live until, once more, African family generosity came into play. Evelyn's sister and brother-in-law and their two children lived in three tiny rooms, and they gave up one room to the newlyweds.

After a while, Nelson and Evelyn were allocated their own municipal house. It was their turn to perform family duties. One of Mandela's sisters moved in with them, and they put her through school. Then Mandela's mother came to stay.

## Family life

There was always a stream of visitors from the Transkei who stayed for as long as they wanted to. Somehow the house always seemed to be big enough for everyone—even when, the following year, Evelyn gave birth to the Mandelas' first child, a son. Nelson and Evelyn would eventually have another son and two daughters, but their first daughter died when she was just nine months old.

Mandela enjoyed family togetherness. He liked to come home at night and to bathe the babies. There were many other things to do, though. He was interested in physical fitness—which would prove to be a lifelong devotion, and early every morning, before anyone was stirring in the streets, he jogged for a few miles. He also liked to go to a gym, and he took up boxing.

While Evelyn worked as a nurse to support the family, Mandela continued his law studies at the University of the Witwatersrand. Most of the students there were white. There were only a few black students, and they had to be exceptional to get into the school. Even then, they had second-class status. They attended classes and lectures but could not take part in sports or social activities. Still, the University of Witwatersrand, like Cape Town University, did, at least, admit black students. Most other "white" universities did not.

Mandela was studying for a second degree, a bachelor of law, so that he could work as a lawyer. He struggled to cope. One of his professors criticized an essay he had written, and an upset Mandela confided to a fellow-student, "I'd like to see how he would manage writing essays by oil lamp at night in a location."

In fact, it was a lot tougher than that. Life in the townships was basic. Like most others, Mandela and his family were packed into a tiny house; its total size was about that of a large living room in a house in Europe or the United States. It did not have hot water or a modern toilet.

It took a lot of time to get to and from the university because of inadequate bus service. Even when he was inside the city, Mandela could not get on just any

*Crowded conditions were common in the townships, where basics such as hot water, modern toilets, and electricity were often lacking. This family of 25 lived in a four-room house.*

bus. He had to wait for the special ones designated for "nonwhites." Mandela dropped out of the degree program and instead studied for examinations to work as a solicitor.

## African Nationalists

Walter Sisulu's second major influence on Nelson Mandela was to introduce him to the ANC. Mandela soon began to work actively with a group of young men whose goal was to promote the organization into a mode of radical action.

These young men were African Nationalists who believed that black people had to be mobilized for outright confrontation with the white rulers. They argued for "noncollaboration"—for black people to refuse to take part in segregated bodies created by the government. They said, for example, that black residents should refuse to sit on "advisory boards" for locations. This was because the boards had no power and were only intended to accept the decisions made

*Racial signs were common due to apartheid. Those below reflect the segregation a black ("Native") would experience when using public transportation.*

by the white officials who ran the locations.

The African Nationalists also opposed black cooperation with people of other groups. They singled out for special suspicion the white and Asian people who were members of the Communist Party. They rejected communism as an alien ideology.

## The ANC Youth League

At a meeting in Johannesburg in 1944, the African Nationalists set up the ANC Youth League. It became the main force that pushed for change inside the parent body.

At the same time, Nelson Mandela had begun to move in other, contradictory circles. Despite the restrictions on the social life of black students at the university, he was meeting whites and Asians whom the Youth League opposed. He found that he liked them as people and enjoyed the intense political discussions he had with them. The friendships he made were deep and lasting.

He plunged into avid debates about how best to achieve freedom for the black majority. His mind, trained and sharpened by his legal studies, made him a natural leader—and even more so when allied with the warmth that, by now, was characteristic of him. By 1948, Mandela was a recognized figure in the Youth League, and he was elected to the key position of general secretary.

This was also a watershed year for South Africa. Nothing would be the same after it. In May, the Afrikaner National Party, led by Dr. D.F. Malan, was voted into office and became the new government.

The Afrikaner Nationalists were elected by the overwhelmingly white electorate because they promised to extend the racial segregation that was already so much a part of South Africa. The aim was nakedly summed up in the Afrikaans word *baaskap*—"to be the boss." Whites were the bosses.

## Racial "pigeonholes"

The new government immediately put its policies into practice. At the heart of the Nationalist agenda was the Population Registration Act. This act put

*Signs such as this one, which used a negative name for blacks, were put up by some white citizens.*

25

every single person into an official classification, which ranged from white through colored, Asian, and Chinese. Every black person was "classified"—that was the official term—according to tribe.

Because people had intermarried for hundreds of years, every person's racial category was not always clear. So, special racial classification boards investigated "borderline" cases. For a time, officials used some strange methods to make their determinations. For example, they might push a pencil through a person's hair to test how "crinkly" it was—the crinklier, the more "colored" the person was. Fingernails were also examined, because it was believed that these, too, showed how "colored" a person was. Racial checks were based on physical appearance, friends, and work.

Racial classifications opened the way to snooping and victimization. Malicious individuals sometimes reported "colored" people to the authorities. Families were split: One person would be classified white, whereas a brother or sister would be declared "colored." When this happened, members of the same family were not allowed to live together.

Racial laws made sexual relations and marriage illegal between people of different groups. The Group Areas Act divided every inch of the country into segregated residential and business areas; only people of a specified race could live or own a business in a certain area.

As experience was to show, time and again, white people grabbed the best land for themselves and ordered blacks, "coloreds," and Asians to live somewhere else. More than 3.5 million people were deprived of their homes, farms, and shops in this way. Armed policemen dealt with anyone who resisted the forced move.

## Enforcing apartheid

Apartheid was enforced on every train and bus in the country. Signs went up everywhere in Afrikaans and English: "Slegs blankes"—"whites only." Black work-

*Black people were forced to carry a pass, similar to a passport, with them at all times.*

ers were not permitted to go on strike. The pass laws were made tougher and the number of arrests of blacks soared. Apartheid was applied to universities to restrict black students. City parks were closed to all nonwhites, as were libraries.

The beaches on the seashore were also segregated. Usually the best—and the safest—beaches were reserved for whites. Concert halls and cinemas were closed to people who were not white, even in those few parts of the country where such strict segregation had not been previously applied. Some jobs, such as house painting and carpentry, were ordered to be for white workers only. Job reservation was now reinforced by new laws.

In education, the government decreed not only separate schools, but also a special educational program for blacks. Dr. H.F. Verwoerd, who later became prime minister, said bluntly that if a black pupil "in any kind of school in existence is being taught to expect that he will live his adult life under a policy of equal rights, he is making a big mistake. There is no place for him in the European community above the level of certain forms of labor."

To deal with opposition, the government enacted the Suppression of Communism Act. This law banned the Communist Party and gave the government power to ban other organizations—and people. Over the years, many hundreds of people would be "banned." This meant that their personal liberty was severely restricted, even though many were actually anticommunist.

Harsh as this law was, it was just the first in a chain of statutes intended to curb opposition. The laws eventually allowed the government to arrest whomever it pleased and to keep people in jail without trial for as long as it wanted.

*Mandela was a busy lawyer. He helped clients protect themselves from racial laws.*

## Suppression picks up pace

As the process of suppression quickly expanded, Mandela played a key role in the ANC Youth League. As general secretary, he helped put the organization on a national footing. The immediate first aim was achieved—to make the Youth League an effective pressure group inside the ANC. By the end of 1949, it convinced the ANC national conference to adopt the "Program of Action"—an outline of plans to oppose white rule based on noncollaboration.

Mandela's views seemed to be in a state of flux at this time. He shared the unease of many Youth League leaders about joining with the Asian community to make a joint stand against racism. Mandela distrusted Asians as being in league with whites. Yet, he had begun to change as he met people of different racial groups and outlooks.

The events of May 1, 1950, were a turning point for him. That day, the Communist Party called a strike to protest the government's intention to ban it. Some ANC leaders backed the strike, arguing that a threat to the Communists was a threat to all. Others, and especially Youth Leaguers, opposed any form of alliance with the Communists.

On the morning of the strike, Mandela is said to have rushed around, urging blacks to go to work. The strike proved to be only moderately successful—but it proved to be memorable because violence broke out and the police opened fire, killing 18 people.

The incident inflamed feelings among those who opposed the government. A new call was issued for a day of protest on June 26, and this time the ANC gave greater support. Mandela wholeheartedly supported the protest and was appointed volunteer-in-chief—the main organizer. He became even more willing to accept ANC cooperation with other groups.

## Mandela the leader

Mandela had begun to rise rapidly to the upper ranks of ANC leadership. In 1951, he was elected president of the Youth League. In 1952, at age 33, he became

"In July [1950] Nelson was jerked out of bed in a predawn police raid. His house was surrounded by the police. The net was cast wide. The homes of twenty other Transvaal activists were raided. They were all arrested. This was the first instance of a Nationalist technique which would become commonplace in the years to come."

—Fatima Meer, from her biography of Mandela, *Higher than Hope*

"Nelson's day was taken up by the court, so he spent the evenings, and late nights, attending to his legal practice and ANC work. As a result he usually returned home when the clock had started counting in the new day; in addition, he rarely spent weekends with the family."

—Fatima Meer, from her biography of Mandela, *Higher than Hope*

president of the powerful Transvaal province, which had Johannesburg as its headquarters. At the national level, he was one of the four deputy presidents of the league.

He also saw progress in his professional life. He and Oliver Tambo, a fellow member of the ANC Youth League, formed a legal partnership. The firm of Mandela and Tambo had its offices in a small building across the street from the Johannesburg magistrates' courts. The waiting room was always full of people sitting quietly until their turn came.

It was quite an achievement to get the offices because, under apartheid, black people were not allowed to occupy offices in the city. They had to go to black areas—even if, for lawyers, that meant being miles away from the main courts. In fact, the government ordered Mandela and Tambo to leave their city offices as their presence infringed the Group Areas Act. They appealed and somehow obtained permission to stay.

There were only a handful of black lawyers in South Africa and life was not easy for them. Even the magistrates did not give them equal respect in open court.

## Challenging the government

Despite his success as a lawyer, Nelson Mandela did not have much time to run his legal practice. He was again appointed volunteer-in-chief for the ANC's next major challenge to the government, the most ambitious in its history. It called for the scrapping of six "unjust laws." The government refused, and the ANC launched a Defiance Campaign: All South Africans were urged to go against racial laws, get arrested, and go to prison.

More than 8,000 people responded to this call during the next few months. Some sat on "whites-only" park benches. Black and Asian protesters entered post offices through "whites-only" doors, and a white volunteer broke the law by going into a location without permission.

Mandela himself was arrested, but he paid bail so that he could continue to organize the campaign. He went up and down South Africa and spoke at hundreds of meetings, small and large. He urged people to defy the law and emphasized that it was a nonviolent protest.

Nonviolence was a deeply held principle of the ANC. ANC leaders believed in peaceful protest because of their Christian outlook. They were also influenced by their contact with the South African Indian Congress and the lessons of resistance taught by Mohandas "Mahatma" Gandhi, who had fought against racial discrimination in South Africa early in the century. He had pioneered the method of nonviolent direct action that freed India from British rule. Nonviolence was also practical politics. The South African police

*This photo shows police beating black demonstrators. The ANC worked to stop racial injustice imposed by apartheid and enforced by police.*

"You must defend the right of African parents to decide the kind of education that shall be given to their children. Teach the children that Africans are not one iota inferior to Europeans. Establish your own community schools where the right kind of education will be given to our children. If it becomes dangerous or impossible to have alternative schools, then you must make every home, every shack, every rickety structure a center of learning for our children. Never surrender to the inhuman and barbaric theories of Verwoerd."

—Nelson Mandela, at the ANC's Transvaal Conference, 1953

carried guns and were quick to shoot. Mandela and the ANC did not want to give them any pretext to open fire. Despite Mandela's best efforts, violence did erupt, from both the police and location people.

The campaign was called off when the government enacted a law that made defiance of apartheid a far more serious crime. Under the new law, someone who sat on the "wrong" park bench, for example, could be imprisoned for five years instead of only a few weeks as had been the case before. People who persuaded others to break the law could be jailed and even lashed with a whip.

## Mass police raids

In what was to become a familiar pattern in the years to come, the Security Police carried out mass raids on homes and offices of ANC and Indian Congress officials. They seized many documents. Later, they arrested 22 leaders, Mandela among them, and charged them with the promotion of communism. At their trial, the accused were found guilty. The judge, however, said that he acknowledged that they had consistently tried to avoid violence, and he sentenced them to jail for only nine months—and suspended the sentences.

Mandela was now truly in the firing line. With other leaders, he was a target for the government. He was among the scores of leaders harassed even though the government did not bother to go to court. Using its dictatorial powers, the government ordered them not to attend any meetings. Mandela was also ordered not to leave Johannesburg.

The gag on him was only partly successful. He wrote a speech that was read for him at the ANC's 1953 regional conference. His speech revealed a great deal about the difficulties protesters faced as they opposed the government: "The masses had to be prepared and made ready for new forms of political struggle," he said. "We had to recuperate our strength and muster our forces for another and more powerful offensive against the enemy. To have gone ahead blindly as if nothing had happened would have been suicidal and stupid.

"The old methods of bringing about mass action through public mass meetings, press statements and leaflets, calling upon people to go to action, have become extremely dangerous and difficult to use effectively."

For some time to come, however, the ANC relied more on words than on mass organization. It continued to be the victim of government action. In the 1950s, black people hoped that the Afrikaner Nationalists could be defeated if enough peaceful protests and pressures could be staged, and the ANC kept to that course.

The effects of 300 years of prejudice, intensified by apartheid, could be seen among both white and black people. Jules Browde, a white friend of Mandela, remembers that he told Mandela how he and his wife were going out one night and their four-year-old boy, who was supposed to be looked after by their black maid, cried, "I don't want to be left with a black face."

"We don't know why he speaks like that," the friend told Mandela. "We are liberal people and there is no trace of racism in our home."

Mandela told him he had been in the same situation—in reverse—with one of his children. White friends had recently visited him at home, and when they left his child said: "Why do you have white people here?"

Mandela said he had replied: "Not all white people have white hearts. Some have black hearts."

## How to fight back?

It was a troubled time for the ANC. The government was all-powerful. More and more, no one could stand up to it as it forged ahead with apartheid. Its latest drive, in the early 1950s, was to take over the education of black children and to ensure that their education was inferior.

The churches, which had done so much for black education, had to decide whether to cooperate with the government. The Methodist Church was among those that refused. Most of Healdtown, Mandela's old

*In 1952, Mandela and other leaders were arrested for promoting communism. He received a nine-month suspended sentence.*

*Above: As in society in general, conditions for black and white workers at gold mines differed dramatically. Blacks lived in crowded rooms and "men-only" compounds.*

*Opposite: Whites were offered cheap rents on houses.*

school, was closed down; its fine buildings were left to decay slowly into ruin.

Mandela faced the dilemma of how to fight back against the new "Bantu education." The ANC acted in line with his call for action and declared an indefinite boycott of schools. It was ill-prepared for such a big step, though. Many parents wanted alternate schooling for their children before they would go along with the boycott. The few who boycotted paid a heavy price. To punish them, .the government denied them readmission to school. It would, incidentally, be 20 years before children adopted school boycotts as a tactic—with far-reaching effects that were seen from 1976 right through the 1980s.

## Banned

Mandela's active political role seemed to come to an end at age 35, in September 1953. A set of banning

orders not only confined him to Johannesburg, but instructed him to resign from the ANC and a host of other organizations. He was also forbidden to attend gatherings. He could not go to political meetings or even social events such as dinner parties or dances.

Although his public presence was curbed, Mandela refused to recognize the validity of the bannings. That was the ANC's attitude, too. The government had begun to ban many leaders, and the ANC responded with the slogan: "We stand by our leaders." In practice, this meant that, whenever a leader was banned, he or she duly resigned from the organization—but secretly remained a committee member. This was a big risk for Mandela and the others. They could be jailed if caught.

As he worked behind the scenes and took care to hide his activities from the Security Police and its network of informers, Mandela took part in the planning

*The Freedom Charter*

*The people shall govern!*

*All national groups shall have equal rights!*

*The people shall share in the country's wealth!*

*The land shall be shared among those who work it!*

*All shall be equal before the law!*

*All shall enjoy equal human rights!*

*There shall be work and security!*

*The doors of learning and of culture shall be opened!*

*There shall be houses, security and comfort!*

*There shall be peace and friendship!*

*Let all who love their people and their country now say, as we say here: "These freedoms we will fight for, side by side, throughout our lives, until we have won our liberty."*

TREASON TRIAL

The
ACCUSED

DECEMBER
1956

of a Congress of the People. Held in Johannesburg on June 26, 1955, this meeting brought thousands of people together. Mandela, in disguise, watched the meeting and the preparation of the "Freedom Charter" from a house nearby.

On the second day of the congress, he saw the police storm in, seize every document they could find, and working into the night, question everyone present. Despite this interruption, the meeting unanimously approved the now-famous Freedom Charter, which set forth demands for a democratic South Africa.

## The treason trial

Looked at today, the charter was a mild and moderate document that set out elementary rights and hopes. To the government at the time, however, it was dangerous and subversive. The government took nearly 18 months to strike back. Then, before dawn on a December day in 1956, Mandela was awakened by heavy knocking on his front door. It was a squad of armed policemen. They searched his home and arrested him. He was one of 156 people arrested. All were charged with high treason. If found guilty, they could be hanged.

By the end of the month, the accused were released on bail, but the trial dragged on and on. The team of prosecutors tried to prove that the accused had worked to overthrow the government and replace it with a Communist state. Almost the entire leadership of the ANC and its allies were pinned down by the trial, since they had to spend every weekday in court, and after each session spent hours in consultation with their lawyers. The trial lasted four and a half years.

## Winnie

Those years saw the transformation of South Africa—and of Mandela's life. In 1956, his marriage to Evelyn had ended. His good looks, charm, and charisma attracted women. Word reached his wife about his friendships with other women. She left

"The [Freedom] Charter is more than a mere list of demands for democratic reforms. It is a revolutionary document precisely because the changes it envisages cannot be won without breaking up the economic and political setup of present South Africa. To win the demands calls for the organization, launching and development of mass struggle on the widest scale."

—Nelson Mandela

"This marriage will be no bed of roses; it is threatened from all sides and only the deepest love will preserve it. . . . Be like your husband, become like his people, and as one with them."

—Winnie Mandela's father, Kokani, at the Mandelas' wedding

Mandela (middle of third row from bottom) was one of 156 people arrested in December 1956 on treason charges.

*Social worker Winnie Nomzano Mdikizela and Nelson Mandela (shown on their wedding day) married in 1958.*

him, and their three children later went to live with her.

There was not much free time left for Mandela, between the treason trial, secret ANC meetings, work at his legal practice at night and on weekends, and exercise whenever possible. Still, after his separation, Nelson was introduced to a young social worker, Winnie Nomzano Mdikizela—and she became part of his hectic schedule.

When they decided to marry in 1958, they had to get police permission because Winnie wanted a traditional ceremony held at her home in the Transkei. Mandela was given permission to leave Johannesburg for four days.

"I knew when I married him that I married the struggle, the liberation of my people," Winnie said. That early understanding helped sustain her in the hard years that followed. She had to get used to the way that he was accessible to people. Wherever he was—walking in the street or eating in a restaurant—

people would come up to him, either merely to say hello, or to seek his help. He always listened. Each person was made to feel that he or she had Mandela's total attention. Everyone was treated with respect.

## The ANC splits

More immediate problems concerned a growing crisis inside the ANC. Although Mandela had come to accept interracial cooperation, some African Nationalist colleagues grew more alarmed as the ANC's ties deepened with other racially separate bodies. All of them wanted to achieve a multiracial South Africa, but each had its own organization.

The African Nationalists argued that the ANC did not give strong enough opposition to apartheid and that it had deserted the "Program of Action" and noncollaboration. The African Nationalists also condemned the Freedom Charter as a meaningless stunt, inspired by the left.

Their grievances gathered strength because the absence of leaders from public positions as a result of bannings and trials meant that less qualified people were in charge. Administration and finances were often a mess.

In August 1958, the disputes finally led Robert Mangaliso Sobukwe to break away from the ANC. Sobukwe had worked with Mandela in the Youth League. The Pan-Africanist Congress (PAC) was formed.

## Fighting the passes

The pass laws that required black men to carry an identity document were being ferociously applied, with hundreds of arrests each day. They were now also enforced on black women.

To black people, the pass was a badge of slavery. Only black people had to have a pass, and only black people were arrested on the spot if they did not show their pass to a policeman. The laws were enforced so harshly that people were arrested while they stood outside their own homes, even if they protested that their pass was just a few feet away.

*Mandela burns his identity pass to protest government repression.*

39

Sobukwe's new PAC accused the ANC of not taking concrete action to fight back. Sobukwe announced the launch of "decisive action," a program in which he called on blacks to leave their passes at home and to offer themselves for arrest.

## The Sharpeville Massacre

Sobukwe led the way on Monday, March 21, 1960. In only a few places did large numbers respond to his call. In the PAC stronghold of Sharpeville, near Johannesburg, the police opened fire on an unarmed crowd and mowed down 69 people.

The massacre put South Africa on newspaper front pages everywhere. Inside the country, it set off a wave of mass anger. Mandela was among the ANC leaders who publicly burnt their passes. The ANC called for a protest strike a week later and drew the biggest response ever known.

As violence erupted, the police shot more people. In Cape Town's locations, the police went from door to door and beat people to force them to return to work. The government declared a state of emergency, which enabled it to do whatever it wanted. It banned the ANC and PAC and arrested thousands. Mandela, still involved in the treason trial, was among the political leaders seized and kept in jail without trial for nearly five months.

The banned organizations went underground. It was hazardous. Merely to be found with an ANC or PAC lapel badge could lead to 12 months in jail.

Many black leaders were totally disillusioned. They had adhered to nonviolence for so many years, "knocking in vain, patiently, moderately and modestly at a closed and barred door," as the ANC's last legal president, Chief Albert Luthuli, put it. They were ignored, were banned, jailed or driven out of the country; or, as had happened at Sharpeville, innocent demonstrators were shot down.

Even so, Mandela again tried nonviolence. He led the planning for a campaign to demand a national convention of all South Africans to prepare a new, just constitution. In May 1961, hundreds packed into a hall in the town of Pietermaritzburg in Natal for a conference. There, they heard a surprise keynote speaker—Nelson Mandela.

No one had realized that his banning orders had expired. He had been out of the limelight for so long that many in the crowd did not appreciate who he was. He was not a fiery orator and did not arouse the audience, and he left as soon as he had given his speech. The mere fact that he had been present, however, and that he was the leader, stirred up a hornets' nest and the police swarmed. They could not find him.

He continued to court danger as he moved around the country to organize a three-day strike in protest against the government's rejection of a call for a national convention to draft a new constitution.

## The Black Pimpernel

Mandela kept in touch with the public through a few journalists he trusted. He phoned them from tele-

"When a government seeks to suppress a peaceful demonstration of an unarmed people by mobilizing the entire resources of the state, military and otherwise, it concedes powerful mass support for such a demonstration. We plan to make government impossible. . . . I am informed that a warrant for my arrest has been issued and that the police are looking for me. . . . [I] will not give myself up to a government I do not recognize."

—Nelson Mandela

"I have had to separate myself from my dear wife and children, from my mother and sisters, to live as an outlaw in my own land. I have had to close my business, to abandon my profession, and live in poverty and misery, as many of my people are doing. I shall fight the Government side by side with you, inch by inch, and mile by mile, until victory is won. I will not leave South Africa, nor will I surrender. The struggle is my life. I will continue fighting for freedom until the end of my days."

—Nelson Mandela, describing life "underground"

phone booths to read them press statements or he met them at night, wearing a simple disguise. Nelson Mandela, the well-dressed lawyer, became a workingman who melted into the background. If he was nervous about being caught, he did not show it. He was calm and determined to organize the strike. Mandela became famous as the Black Pimpernel, the man the police could not catch.

The government put the police on guard against the three-day strike. Black workers were threatened with loss of their jobs if they stayed away from work. Leaders were arrested. Meetings were prohibited. The massive pressures ensured that the strike was only partly successful.

The extent to which the government went to destroy the strike and to crush the call for a national convention proved to be the last straw for Nelson Mandela. This was the great turning point. As he later revealed, in June 1961, he and some colleagues "came to the conclusion that, as violence in this country was inevitable, it would be unrealistic and wrong for African leaders to continue preaching peace and non-violence at a time when the government met our peaceful demands with force."

He referred to a secret meeting attended by representatives of the ANC and the Communist Party at which it was agreed that nonviolence had proved useless and that there should be a switch to violent resistance. They set up an underground sabotage movement called Umkhonto we Sizwe (Spear of the Nation).

## Sabotage

Umkhonto struck its first blow on December 16, 1961, the day observed by Afrikaners each year to mark victory over the Zulus in a major battle the previous century. The sabotage was aimed at property, such as electricity pylons—and killing people was totally avoided. Only years later would bombs be set off intended to kill people.

A few weeks later, Mandela slipped out of the country. He did not have a passport and went through

As shown in these stills from the movie Mandela, in 1961 the ANC decided they would no longer promote only nonviolent protests. Destruction of property also became acceptable.

Botswana to travel to other African countries, where he met leaders and sought help in the fight against apartheid. He wanted financial aid and training for guerrillas. African states, such as Ghana, listened sympathetically and promised support.

Six months later, Mandela returned to South Africa. He crossed the border illegally from Botswana. The police heard he was back, and the hunt for him was on again.

Mandela's underground base was a luxury farm called Lilliesleaf in Rivonia, outside Johannesburg. Hoping to find Mandela, the police watched Winnie and raided her several times. She managed, under their noses, to visit Mandela with their two daughters, Zindzi and Zeni.

Mandela moved around the country to create the new organization. His disguise was as a chauffeur with the name, "David Motsamai." As he drove out of Durban one Sunday morning, August 5, 1962, however, a police car overtook him and forced him to halt. Two other police cars were behind. They knew who he was; they had been tipped off that he was coming on that road.

The police were excited about their big catch. Mandela was taken to Pretoria and charged with inciting black workers to strike and with leaving the country illegally. He was sentenced to five years in jail. As sentence was passed, he defiantly turned to the packed public gallery, raised his fist and shouted, "Amandla!" (Strength).

## Prison

Prison conditions were rough, and apartheid meant that blacks had it worst of all. Mandela was given a shirt, sandals, and khaki three-quarter-length pants—known as "tsotsi shorts" after *tsotsis*, the word for teenage gangsters in the locations. At that time, black prisoners were not given socks or shoes—and they always had to wear their tsotsi shorts despite the intense winter cold in the prisons.

After a few months, Mandela was driven to Cape Town in a truck with three other political prisoners. It took a night and most of a day. They were handcuffed and shackled to each other, and they were given a bucket for use as a toilet inside the truck. In Cape Town, Mandela was transferred to a boat for an hour's sail to Robben Island, which was then in development as a maximum-security prison.

Mandela was put to work with other prisoners. He sat on the ground in long rows with them and pounded stones into rubble. The task was intended to help build their own new prison on the island to house the rapidly increasing number of black people who were jailed for their efforts against apartheid. Other prisoners cut slate from the quarry, dug lime in another quarry, or collected bird droppings.

Nelson Mandela had not been in prison long when there was a dramatic political development outside. On

*Winnie Mandela leaves court during her husband's 1962 trial.*

July 11, 1963, a dry cleaner's van and a baker's van drove up the long driveway of Lilliesleaf farm in Rivonia. Policemen and dogs raced out of the vans. They arrested 16 people found there, including Walter Sisulu, who had gone underground several months before. The police were triumphant. They had tracked down the high command of Umkhonto we Sizwe.

## Accused Number One

On the basis of documents found at Lilliesleaf, Mandela was brought back to face new charges with nine others in the Supreme Court at Pretoria. He was listed as Accused Number One. The group was charged with sabotage and an attempt to cause a violent revolution.

In a lengthy statement, Mandela set out his thoughts. To explain why he and others had started Umkhonto we Sizwe, he said, "Firstly, we believed that as a result of government policy, violence by the African people had become inevitable, and that unless responsible leadership was given to catalyze and control the feelings of our people, there would be outbreaks of terrorism which would produce an intensity of bitterness and hostility between the various races of this country which is not produced even by war.

"Secondly, we felt that without sabotage there would be no way open to the African people to succeed in their struggle against the principle of white supremacy. All lawful modes of expressing opposition to this principle had been closed by legislation and we were placed in a position in which we had either to accept a permanent state of inferiority, or to defy the government. We chose to defy the government."

## Life

The charges were so grave that Mandela and the others faced the death sentence. Protests rang around the world. No doubt Mandela's unbending, dignified justification of his position had an effect, even in the South African courtroom. Rather than execution, he received a sentence of life imprisonment.

• • • • • • • • • • • • • • • • • • • • • •

**"More powerful than my fear of the dreadful conditions to which I might be subjected is my hatred for the dreadful conditions to which my people are subjected outside prison throughout this country."**

**—Nelson Mandela**

• • • • • • • • • • • • • • • • • • • • • •

*Nelson Mandela's mother, Nosekeni (Fanny) talked to her grandchildren about her son while he was in prison.*

This time, he and those of his fellow prisoners who were blacks and Asians, were flown to Cape Town by military plane to be ferried to Robben Island. There, Nelson Mandela spent the next 18 years. The government had announced that the sentences of political prisoners would not be reduced. Murderers, robbers, and rapists were usually released after serving half or two-thirds of their sentences. That was not the case for political prisoners.

Through the 1960s and most of the 1970s, conditions were harsh. The food was poor, and even the limited rations that Mandela and others were supposed to have—such as a teaspoonful of sugar a day—were not always provided, perhaps because the wardens stole supplies. Mandela slept on a mat on the concrete floor. He had a bucket in his cell to use as a toilet.

There was no radio. No newspapers were allowed; to be caught with even a piece of smuggled newspaper brought punishment. The wardens were vicious. The day began at 5:30 A.M., and the tough discipline subjected Mandela to long hours of silent work. At the end of the working day, he had to strip naked to be searched. After supper, it was a long night in the cell.

Mandela rapidly gained a reputation for his willingness to help others. It did not matter whether a prisoner was an ANC member or was from a rival movement, such as PAC. Mandela was friendly and was available to give advice. Exactly as he had been when a free man, he was renowned for his calmness and for his willingness to listen to what others had to say.

The political prisoners established their own network of committees that dealt with matters that varied from internal discipline to sports and education. Mandela stuck to his own fitness routines. He did push-ups in his cell early in the morning. He also played chess and dominoes and studied successfully for the bachelor of law degree he had not obtained in college in the 1940s.

He grew in stature, and because the authorities recognized and feared it, they separated him and a few prisoners, like Walter Sisulu, from the others and kept them in a separate part of the jail.

## A time of change

Gradually, improvements came about on Robben Island. The food got better, warmer clothing and beds were provided, newspapers and magazines were allowed, and so were radio broadcasts. A new type of prison warden seemed to be taking over.

The change could be seen in an experience Mandela had: Months went by and he did not receive a single letter from Winnie. The officer who censored letters taunted him that Winnie did not write to him because she was not interested in him any more. Then, a new warden took over and Mandela complained about his lack of letters. There was an investigation and it was found that the censor had six letters from Winnie that he had not given to Mandela. The warden promised Mandela it would never happen again.

The easing of prison conditions went along with changes in South Africa's general political situation. Apartheid was still the law and it was rigorously applied. Even so, the Afrikaner Nationalists began to question some of their policies.

## Winnie's struggle

Mandela's pain at his separation from his wife and children was made worse because of the consequences of her struggles for his freedom and her own involvement in politics. She was banned and had to obtain permission each time she wanted to visit him. It was an expensive trip—Cape Town is 950 miles from Johannesburg.

For 18 months, she could not visit Mandela because she was detained and held without trial. She was then charged under the Terrorism Act. That could have led to the death penalty, but she was acquitted. She was constantly harassed. The police raided her home at all times of the day and night and she was also terrorized by men who attacked her.

Then she was banished to the location of the village of Brandfort, 200 miles south of Johannesburg. She could not leave without permission. She had no telephone. Her "office" became a public telephone booth

> "[Mandela] stood head and shoulders above the others. Everyone looked up to him and respected him. When he spoke, we listened. He was patient, tolerant and I never saw him lose his temper."
>
> —Strini Moodley, a prisoner on Robben Island

*While Nelson Mandela was in prison, Winnie Mandela, who shared her husband's political beliefs, was harassed by the government.*

in the village; twice a day, she went there to phone people and to receive calls from friends. Like her husband, she could not have anything she said published.

On June 16, 1976, black opposition finally exploded. An order that black schools had to make greater use of the Afrikaans language sparked widespread protests. It was called the Children's Revolt. In response, the police carried out shootings. By the end of the year, hundreds of people, most of them schoolchildren, had been killed.

Afterward, South Africa was plagued by protest. Sometimes it receded for a few months, only to surge

One of the victims of the Children's Revolt against apartheid is pictured above.
Bottom, left: Violence spread as shops and government buildings were set on fire.

*After the Children's Revolt, South Africa experienced years of protests by various groups.*

again. The protests, with their demands for change, helped bring Mandela's name before the public again. For many years, he had been largely forgotten. Slowly, however, word began to get out to South Africa and the rest of the world about the strength of character of the man on Robben Island.

## Release offers for Mandela

The government was among the first to recognize the danger the protests posed. Even before the 1976 Children's Revolt, Mandela was quietly told that he could leave jail as long as he left the country. He was told that he could go to the Transkei, one of the tribal mini-states that was considered independent. Mandela refused.

Throughout the 1970s, at least four or five offers followed. Each time, Mandela insisted that he would only leave prison if no conditions were placed on him. When released, he intended to be a free man, who could do whatever he wanted.

The few people who were allowed to visit him—whether friends or dignitaries—spoke about his courage and wisdom and the contribution that he should be permitted to make to resolve the deepening racial crisis in South Africa.

Recognition of Mandela's struggle began to spread. Universities, city councils, and trade unions in many parts of the world began to show their respect for him by giving him degrees, naming streets and squares after him, and starting scholarships in his honor. Governments, political parties, and international organizations started to call for his release.

## To Pollsmoor Prison

Nelson Mandela's conditions changed radically. In 1982, after 18 years on Robben Island, he was suddenly told that he would be leaving in half an hour. With Sisulu and a few others, he was taken to Pollsmoor—a prison set in beautiful farm surroundings near the city of Cape Town. No explanation was given. Perhaps the government feared that Mandela and his colleagues had become too powerful on the island.

Mandela's growing status was further acknowledged by the government: He had to go into hospital for an operation, and when discharged, he went back to Pollsmoor—but into a private cell.

The minister of justice began to visit him. They liked each other and their lengthy discussions were friendly. The wardens were respectful to him, even as they unlocked gates inside the jail for him to pass through.

Even with all this, though, he was still a man deprived of his liberty. Pollsmoor was a maximum security prison and Mandela's cell faced inward; all he could see were the grim interior walls and a patch of sky above. As a Christmas treat, he was taken onto the prison grounds and allowed to walk on grass. It was an exciting moment: For the first time in 20 years, he was able to touch grass.

## Release—but on condition

In January 1985, South Africa's president, P.W. Botha, brought the issue of Nelson Mandela's release into the open when he publicly made an offer to him. On the surface it seemed reasonable: Mandela simply had to renounce violence. Apartheid was still in place, however,

"Police massacres of blacks had punctuated South Africa's history but nothing so terrible had been known: a modern armed force moving against schoolchildren."

—Mary Benson, South African author

*A rock concert was held on July 11, 1988, at London's Wembley Stadium to celebrate Mandela's seventieth birthday.*

and the ANC was still waging its armed struggle against white rule. For Mandela to condemn violence would be to condemn the ANC and its struggle for freedom.

He wrote a statement, and his daughter, Zindzi, read it to a public meeting in Soweto: "I am not less life-loving than you," he said. "But I cannot sell my birthright, nor am I prepared to sell the birthright of the people to be free." He would only negotiate with the government when he was a free man and the ANC was free. "I cannot and will not give any undertaking at a time when I and you, the people, are not free. Your freedom and mine cannot be separated. I will return."

Worldwide demands for his release continued to be heard. He represented freedom for South Africa's people and became the symbol for freedom all over the world where people were oppressed.

## Split inside government

A split developed inside the South African government. Mandela was a terrible embarrassment. He kept international attention focused on apartheid and on the unceas-

"We are celebrating the seventieth birthday of the world's most famous political prisoner. Since his imprisonment in August 1962 Nelson Rolihlahla Mandela has embodied the struggle for freedom in South Africa. In that country it is illegal to quote him or to display his portrait yet there is no doubt that most South Africans—among them young people born long after he vanished into jail—regard him as their authentic leader."

—From "Nelson Mandela 70th Birthday Tribute"

"Internationally he has been widely honored: by students and faculties of universities; by cities in Scotland and Italy, in Greece and Australia, which conferred 'freedom' on him. Streets, parks, buildings and squares have been named after him. Poems and songs extol his life. Many heads of governments and 2,000 Mayors in 53 countries call for his release."

—From "Nelson Mandela 70th Birthday Tribute"

ing violence as the white government kept itself in power by force. Some members of the government did not want to release him out of fear of what a freed Mandela might do. Others argued that they had no choice.

The world's media gave Mandela avid attention. Every report of his imminent release was hotly pursued. His seventieth birthday, on July 18, 1988, was observed as no birthday has ever been. The highlight was a rock concert at London's Wembley Stadium that featured the greatest stars, watched live by millions of people in 28 countries.

Then, suddenly, it was announced that Mandela was ill. As alarm swept the world, he was taken to the hospital with tuberculosis. He recovered and was placed in a comfortable house at the Victor Verster Prison near Cape Town. He rejected the offer to have his family come to live with him; he did not want them with him in jail. Despite the comfort of his new surroundings, he was on his own most of the time, and his loneliness was acute.

In 1989, political events picked up speed. South Africa's economy was reeling under the impact of the nearly nonstop internal turbulence, combined with the effects of sanctions applied by other countries. As 1990 began, and with recently elected president of South Africa F. W. de Klerk, it was obvious that Mandela's release was only a question of time.

On February 2, 1990, de Klerk accepted the pressures for change in South Africa and announced the unbanning of the African National Congress, the Pan-Africanist Congress, and all the other bodies that had been made illegal over the years.

## Release—at last

Finally, on February 10, he announced that Nelson Mandela was to be released the next day—without any conditions. That was why the hundreds of journalists were outside Victor Verster Prison on a hot summer's afternoon, and why a huge crowd gathered outside Cape Town's city hall for the first sight of the man many in South Africa revered as the leader who would bring them to freedom.

Mandela spoke of peace, democracy, and freedom. He ended with a declaration that his commitment was unchanged: "In conclusion, I wish to quote my own words during my trial of 1964. They are as true today as they were then:

> I have fought against white domination and I have fought against black domination. I have carried the ideal of a democratic and free society in which all persons live together in harmony and with equal opportunity. It is an ideal which I hope to live for and to achieve. But, if need be, it is an ideal for which I am prepared to die."

His words made abundantly clear that his release from prison was not an end, but a beginning. Without delay, Mandela met with leaders of the government and the first formal talks between the ANC and the government were held. The two sides set up a joint working group to deal with practical problems, such as how to decide when political prisoners should be released from jail and whether exiles might return.

*Opposite, top: Mandela spoke to cheering crowds at a rally two days after his release from 27 years of imprisonment.*

*Opposite, bottom: The night he regained his freedom, supporters cheered.*

## Without bitterness

As Mandela moved from one meeting to another, what startled many people, whites in particular, was his lack of bitterness about the past. He showed sympathy for the anxieties of white people about their future as a minority group, subject to majority rule.

Mandela worked hard as he traveled widely to raise funds for the ANC and to personally thank the various governments that had added to the call for his release. He was deputy president, but effectively he was now in charge of the organization. He persuaded colleagues on the ANC's National Committee to hold talks with the government in an attempt to pave the way for constitutional negotiations. He was now able to convince the more aggressive elements in the ANC to talk and to suspend their armed struggle.

Nelson Mandela and F.W. de Klerk developed a strong chemistry. They were jointly nominated for the Nobel Peace Prize, and although they did not win, they did share other international human rights awards.

Negotiations pressed forward and de Klerk repealed discriminatory legislation, such as the Reservation of Separate Amenities Act, the Lands Act, and the Group Areas Act. It was a time of hope and friendship among the people of Africa. Interracial violence was almost nonexistent. Expectations were high.

## Winnie

In July 1991, Mandela was elected ANC president and began to prepare for the start of negotiations by the Convention for a Democratic South Africa, CODESA. Mandela continued to be peaceful, firm, and charismatic. The ANC rallied behind him, and the government leaders were able to talk with him. If Nelson Mandela's professional life was relatively smooth, however, all was not well in his personal life.

According to rumors, Winnie Mandela was involved in a relationship with her deputy in the ANC's social welfare department, and eventually, Mandela moved out of their family home. Controversy continued to follow Winnie, and new press reports alleged that she

may have been involved in the murder of teenage activist Stompie Moeketsi. Throughout this trying period, Nelson Mandela stood by his wife and steadfastly proclaimed her innocence.

At the same time, however, he was under considerable pressure from the ANC to distance himself from his wife because of the political embarrassment she was causing. Eventually, Mandela relented. Although he still loved Winnie, Mandela announced, irreconcilable differences had arisen between them and they planned to separate. This was a tremendously difficult and painful time for Mandela. The press—and all of South Africa—recognized that the main political issues were far more important and the Mandelas' personal troubles had very little effect on opinions and events.

## Violence stirs fears

The CODESA talks were fraught with problems. The economy was in a poor state, big business needed some security before it could invest, and the ANC and government could not agree upon terms. Despite Mandela's private talks with de Klerk, negotiations fell through.

Violence increased—not between whites and blacks but between different black groups, mainly between the ANC and the Zulu movement, Inkatha. This played into the hands of white antireformists and stirred fears in everyone. There were accusations that the violence was paid for and engineered by the security forces and

*Opposite: Hundreds of thousands of New Yorkers welcomed Mandela with a parade. He stopped in New York City during a series of visits to world capitals after his release from prison.*

*F. W. de Klerk, South Africa's president (pictured with Mandela), decided to release Mandela from jail.*

that the government was therefore responsible. When the government denied this and took no action, it lost credibility and the trust of the people. Many came to believe that de Klerk did not really intend to make peace and wanted to make the ANC look like violent aggressors. Whatever the truth, the situation undermined CODESA and the talks failed.

## Power struggle

The huge changes that occurred after Mandela's release showed the great desire among whites and blacks for change and cooperation. The failure was in the struggle for power and the difficulty of creating a completely new government.

Among black people, support for Mandela was as strong as ever. Still, his personal authority was unable to quell the violent struggle for supremacy between the ANC and Inkatha.

Despite these initial problems, race relations did improve, and government changes were made. In 1991, Nelson Mandela was elected president of the ANC at the organization's first national conference since it was banned. Then, in 1993, Nelson Mandela was awarded the Nobel Peace Prize in recognition of his work to help all the South Africans who had suffered and struggled for freedom through the years of apartheid.

Mandela's biggest achievement, however, came in 1994, when he became the first democratically elected president of South Africa. He served from May 1994 to June 1999. In 1998, as he neared the end of his time in office, he married Graca Machel, a renowned activist from Mozambique, who is known for her efforts to help women and children around the world.

In 1999, Mandela retired from public life and moved back to his boyhood home in Qunu. Although he remains out of the international spotlight, he continues to take an interest in the affairs of his nation and he remains an enduring symbol of South Africa's successful struggle for democracy.

# Timeline

| | |
|---|---|
| 1652 | The first permanent white settlement is founded at the Cape. |
| 1795 | Great Britain takes over occupation of the Cape. |
| 1834 | The Great Trek starts: more than 10,000 Afrikaners leave the Cape Colony. |
| 1899 | The Boer War breaks out and continues until 1902. |
| 1910 | May 31: The Union of South Africa is formed. Black people are not included in the negotiations and are given second-class status. |
| 1912 | The African National Congress (ANC) is founded. |
| 1913 | The Native Land Act is passed: only 7.3 percent of land is reserved for black people. |
| 1918 | July 18: Nelson Rolihlahla Mandela is born in Qunu in the Transkei region of South Africa. |
| 1938 | Nelson Mandela enrolls at the South African Native College at Fort Hare. |
| 1941 | Nelson Mandela is suspended by the college authorities for participation in a strike. He goes to Johannesburg, where Walter Sisulu introduces him to the ANC. |
| 1942 | Nelson Mandela earns his bachelor of arts degree by correspondence. He enrolls at the University of Witwatersrand to study law, but does not complete the course. |
| 1944 | The ANC Youth League is founded. Nelson Mandela is elected to the Executive Committee. He marries Evelyn Mase. |
| 1948 | Mandela is elected general secretary of the Youth League. The National Party wins the general election and introduces apartheid. |
| 1949 | December: The ANC adopts the Youth League's "Programme of Action." |
| 1950 | The Population Registration Act, the Group Areas Act, and the Suppression of Communism Act are passed and the Communist Party is banned. May 1: The Communist Party calls a strike to protest its banning. The police open fire, killing 18 people. June 26: The ANC, with support from other groups, organizes a day of protest. Mandela is appointed volunteer-in-chief. |
| 1952 | Mandela becomes president of the Transvaal ANC. Mandela is appointed volunteer-in-chief to organize a defiance campaign—a nonviolent protest against the government's unjust laws. 8,500 people break apartheid laws and are jailed. The ANC's membership increases from 7,000 to 100,000. Mandela and Oliver Tambo go into partnership as lawyers. |
| 1953 | September: Mandela is banned and instructed to resign from the ANC and not to attend any political meetings. |
| 1955 | June 26: A Congress of the People is held in Johannesburg. Almost 3,000 delegates attend and approve the Freedom Charter. |
| 1956 | Mandela's marriage to Evelyn Mase ends. December: Mandela is one of 156 charged with high treason. By the end of the treason trial, which lasts over four years, all the defendants are set free. |
| 1958 | June 14: Mandela marries Winnie Nomzano Mdikizela. |
| 1960 | March 21: In the Sharpeville Massacre, the police open fire on unarmed people demonstrating against the pass laws. Sixty-nine demonstrators are killed. |

March 30: A state of emergency is declared. Mandela is imprisoned for five months.

April 8: The ANC and PAC are banned and go underground.

| | |
|---|---|
| 1961 | Umkhonto we Sizwe is set up under Mandela's leadership. |
| 1962 | August 5: After 17 months underground, Mandela is arrested and, in November, is sentenced to five years' imprisonment. |
| 1963 | May 24: Mandela is moved from Pretoria Prison to Robben Island. July 11: Sixteen members of Umkhonto we Sizwe are arrested. October: Mandela is brought back to Pretoria to face further charges. |
| 1964 | June 11: Nelson Mandela is found guilty of sabotage and trying to cause a violent revolution. He is sentenced to life imprisonment and taken back to Robben Island. He spends another 18 years there, and eventually earns his bachelor of law degree. |
| 1973 | Mandela is offered release from jail to the Transkei. He refuses. |
| 1976 | June 16: In Soweto, a demonstration by 1,000 black schoolchildren is fired on by police. The Children's Revolt spreads all over the country and hundreds are killed. |
| 1979 | Mandela is given the Nehru Award by India. |
| 1983 | Mandela is given an honorary degree by the City College of New York. He also receives the Austrian Human Rights Award. |
| 1985 | January: President P. W. Botha offers Mandela release on condition that he renounces violence. He refuses. |
| 1986 | A state of emergency is declared and the Pass Laws are repealed. |
| 1988 | July 18: Mandela's 70th birthday. Shortly after, he contracts tuberculosis. He recovers and is moved to Victor Verster Prison. |
| 1989 | July 4: Mandela meets President F. W. de Klerk. |
| 1990 | February 2: De Klerk repeals the bans on the ANC, PAC, the Communist Party, and other organizations. February 11: After 27 years, Mandela, at age 71, is released from prison. May 2: The first official talks between the ANC and the South African government take place. Both sides commit themselves to peaceful change, but there are continuing outbreaks of violence between Inkatha and the ANC. October: The Separate Amenities Act is repealed. The State of Emergency is lifted completely. |
| 1991 | De Klerk scraps the remaining apartheid laws. December 20—21: Multiparty negotiations begin at the Convention for a Democratic South Africa (CODESA). |
| 1992 | April 13: Mandela announces his separation from his wife, Winnie. May 15—16: CODESA II deadlocks over the issue of the percentages needed for regional government decisions and a proposed bill of rights. May 28—31: The ANC holds a national party conference and calls for supporters to put pressure on the government. June 17: More than 40 people are killed by alleged KwaMadala Hostel dwellers in the township of Biopatong. The ANC suspends negotiations with the government and withdraws from CODESA. |
| 1993 | Mandela receives the Nobel Peace Prize. |
| 1994 | Mandela becomes South Africa's first democratically elected president. |
| 1998 | Mandela marries Graca Machel. |
| 1999 | Mandela retires from public life and moves to Qunu. |

# Glossary

**African National Congress (ANC):** Founded in South Africa in 1912 to campaign for national unity and equal rights for black people. The ANC followed a policy of nonviolence until it was banned by the government in 1960. The movement then went underground and, in 1961, formed a military wing, Umkhonto we Sizwe. The banning order was lifted in February 1990.

**Afrikaans:** A language that developed from Dutch. It is spoken by descendants of the Boers and is one of the two official languages of South Africa (the other is English). Most black people in South Africa refuse to use Afrikaans. The government's ruling that lessons had to be taught in Afrikaans, instead of English, in black schools led to student riots in Soweto in 1976.

**Afrikaner:** A white, Afrikaans-speaking person in South Africa, usually a descendant of the Boers.

**Apartheid:** Literally, "separateness," it is a system of racial segregation. Apartheid became government policy in South Africa in 1948.

**Asian:** In South Africa, someone of Indian or Chinese descent, even if he or she was born in South Africa. The first Indians were brought to work in South Africa by the British in 1860.

**Banning order:** In South Africa, an order the government placed on people it considered a danger to national security. The order restricts, for example, the person's movements and the number of people that person can be with at any one time. A banning order can also be placed on an organization.

**Bantu:** A member of any of the several peoples of central and southern Africa who speak one of the Bantu languages, including Swahili, Xhosa, and Zulu. Until 1978, Bantu was the official South African government name for any black person, but is now considered offensive.

**Black:** In South Africa, the preferred description for all people with brown skin. In recent years, many South African Asians and so-called "colored" people have called themselves black to show solidarity between all oppressed groups. In 1987, out of an estimated total population of 29 million, more than 20 million were black.

**Boer:** Literally a "farmer," the name given to a descendant of Dutch or French Protestant settlers in South Africa.

**Boer War:** Fought between the British and the Boers from 1899 to 1902.

**Boycott:** A campaign in which something or someone is not dealt with, used, or bought as a means of protest.

**"Colored":** In South Africa, the official term for pale brown people considered neither black nor white. Usually these people are of mixed race. The term is regarded as nonsense by opponents of apartheid.

**Communist:** Someone who believes in the theory of common ownership of the means of production, distribution, and supply by a classless society. In such a society, each person works according to his or her ability and receives according to need. In South Africa, many opponents of racism were called Communists and given banning orders.

**Concentration camp:** During the Boer War, a camp where those people not involved in the fighting were housed. Also, a guarded camp for the detention of political prisoners.

**Democracy:** Government by the people, either directly or, more usually, through elected representatives.

**Group Areas Act:** Passed in 1950, the basic legislation that defined where people could live and work according to their race classification.

**Guerrilla:** A person who is not part of any army but still takes part in war activities.

**Location:** A small township.

**Native:** Literally, native means "born in the country." At one time, native was the official term for a black South African. It is now considered offensive.

**Nazism:** The ideology of the National Socialist German Workers' Party, in particular, control of the economy by the state and racial superiority. The party was founded in Germany in 1919 and came to power in 1933 under Adolf Hitler. When World War II broke out in 1939, many Afrikaners were sympathetic to Nazi Germany and voted against South Africa's involvement in the war. When these Afrikaners lost the vote, they regrouped as the National Party.

**Pan-Africanist Congress (PAC):** A militant movement started by a breakaway group of ANC members. The PAC was banned from 1960 to 1990.

**Pass Laws:** The first pass law was introduced in 1809 and it required all Africans to carry a pass when they were off their "master's" property. The laws were extended and strengthened between 1870 and 1980 to ensure that black people lived in the most convenient place for white people. Every black person, age 16 or over, had to carry a pass book and if caught without it, could be fined or imprisoned. These laws were repealed in July 1986.

**Race:** A group that shares a common history, language, ancestry, or geographical area. The concept enables some groups to claim that they are "superior" and can treat other groups as "inferior." Genetic evidence now proves that only minor characteristics, such as differences in hair and skin type, have a biological basis. Differences in talents, personality, and intelligence within any one population group are enormous compared with differences between groups.

**Racism:** The belief that some races are biologically superior. This is used by people to treat other races poorly.

**Sabotage:** An attempt to damage property deliberately.

**Sanctions:** Financial and military measures used by one or several states against another that has broken international law. The intention is to punish the country to force it to change its policy or polities.

**Segregation:** The separation of one group of people from another, usually black people from white people. Under such a system, separate facilities are provided for each group, but usually, those for black people are inferior to those for white people.

**Sisulu, Walter:** A founding member of the ANC Youth League in 1944 who was elected secretary of the ANC in December 1949.

**Sobukwe, Robert:** Leader of the Pan-Africanist Congress (PAC).

**Township:** In South Africa, an area situated on the edge of a large town or city that is set aside for black and "colored" people—mainly workers who serve the white town—to live in. Conditions in the townships were very poor compared with those that many white people enjoyed in the towns.

**Treason:** An attempt to illegally overthrow a government or state to which one owes allegiance.

**Umkhonto we Sizwe:** The militant wing of the ANC led by Nelson Mandela until his imprisonment in 1962. It was set up in 1961 after the ANC was banned by the South African government. Umkhonto we Sizwe means "Spear of the Nation."

**White:** In South Africa, the term used for any resident of European descent with pale brown or pink skin. In 1987, out of an estimated total population of 29 million, 4.9 million were white.

# Index

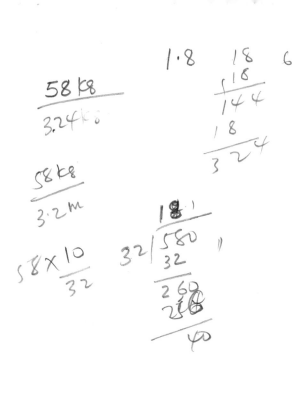

$1 \cdot 8$  $18$  $6$

$\dfrac{58\,kg}{3.24\,kg}$

$\begin{array}{r} 18 \\ \underline{\times 18} \\ 144 \\ 18 \\ \hline 324 \end{array}$

$\dfrac{58\,kg}{3.2\,M}$

$58 \times \dfrac{10}{32}$

$\begin{array}{r} 18 \\ 32\overline{)580} \\ 32 \\ \hline 260 \\ 216 \\ \hline 40 \end{array}$